ADVENTURES OF A
RIDESHARE
DRIVER

ADVENTURES OF A
RIDESHARE
DRIVER

CHARLES A. CAMPISE

ARPress
ILLUMINATING IDEAS
EMPOWERING VOICES

ARPress
45 Dan Road Suite 36
Canton MA 02021

Hotline: 1(800) 220-7660
Fax: 1(855) 752-6001

Ordering Information:
Quantity sales. Special discounts are available on quantity purchases by corporations, associations, and others. For details, contact the publisher at the address above.

Printed in the United States of America.

ISBN-13:   Paperback   979-8-89356-092-3
           eBook   979-8-89356-093-0

Library of Congress Control Number: 2024904580

CONTENTS

This book is dedicated to my loving wife, Rosemary, who listened late at night to all of the stories I brought home from my hours of driving for RIDESHARE. She patiently listened and laughed with me as I recounted the day's and night's adventures taking people from all walks of life to their destinations for work, pleasure or both. I have written this book to give fond memories to people who have visited the Austin region for the first time, for the people who were all of my wonderful passengers, and for people who intend to visit the region in the future. I hope my readers get a few laughs when they read the episodes recounted here. Most of the material is from memories I have of the first three years of my driving as a RIDESHARE driver. Some of the material is taken from the three journals which contain comments from passengers, either in English or in any of twenty-four other languages contained in them. Readers will find in this book some of the stories which I shared with passengers as we traveled from one location to another, recalling some of the history of the region which I shared from my life in the area for the past fifty years.

Readers take note that I am a current driver for more than one rideshare company. I have decided to use a generic term to describe each of those companies. The word 'RIDESHARE' is the word I have chosen to represent those companies.

MY FIRST PHOTO WITH PASSENGERS

I took my first photo with passengers on the evening of my first day as a ride-sharing driver. The location was Austin, Texas. I had just taken two men to the oldest Austin' honky-tonk'. I left them off and got a request from a Mexican food restaurant a few blocks north. I drove into the drive way and stopped at the valet station. Four very tipsy women came staggering out the door and got into the car. They were talking very loudly. The three women in the back seat were so loud that I struggled to hear the woman in the front seat as I spoke with her. I did manage to share with her that this were my first day as a driver. The woman in the front seat told me that they were celebrating their fifth year anniversary of graduation from law school. We got onto Congress Avenue in the downtown area when one of the women in the backseat shouted, "Hey, Driver. When you get to our destination, turn off the car engine and get out of the car with us". (She must have heard me say over all of the commotion that this were my first day as a driver.) Upon arrival at the bar of their choice on Red River Street, I did as she requested. The woman who had shouted immediately got out of the back seat, grabbed a woman who was standing at the front door of the bar, and barked, "Walk over here, take my phone camera, and get us a picture with the new driver. We don't want to miss this opportunity". I certainly hope that I helped them to 'cheer up' as they walked into Cheer Up Charlie's.

MY FIRST ENCOUNTER WITH A FIST FIGHT

This event also took place on the first day(night) of my driving the RIDESHARE car. I had decided to see how much business there was for a ride-share driver in Austin, Texas after two in the morning. I cruised down San Jacinto Street slowly and got a ride request from Seventh Street, parallel to the action on Sixth Street. I had to wade through a mass of taxi cabs that were in line against the curb on Seventh Street. I barely made the turn when four people waved me down. Wow! My first after-hours riders. They hopped into the car quickly to get out of the traffic jam. One guy in the front seat. One guy directly behind him and two women side-by-side. They said that I was taking them to West campus. I worked the car to the far left lane, turned left onto Trinity, went one block north to Eight Street, and realized that the man in the front seat was turning and hitting the man behind him multiple times in the face. The guy in the back seat was trying to fight back by putting a strangle hold on the guy in front. I asked them to stop the action. They did not, so I decided to take matters into my own hands. I got to Eighth Street, went to the next intersection and hooked the car to the right, stopping as abruptly and safely as I were able. As soon as I stopped, I saw red and blue lights flashing in my rear view mirror. It was the LAW!!!. As I thought this to myself, all four passengers shouted in unison, "It's the law!" A state trooper had pulled up behind me. He got out of his cruiser, came to my window and asked for my identification and proof of insurance. The trooper told me that I had turned onto a one way street going in the wrong direction. He read the material as I explained that I was a driver for a ride-sharing company and was taking passengers back home as safely as possible. He then said, "I see that you are not from around here. So, the next time you come to Austin, come before dark, drive the downtown area and learn which one way streets go which way". He then leaned into the car, looking at the guy in the front and then the guy in the back. He said, "Is there a PROBLEM here?" I told him that there had been a minor problem but that I had fixed it. He then said in a very gruff voice, as he looked at the two guys one at a time, "Well, if you can't, THEN, I CAN!" Needless to say, we then took off and continued to West campus in total silence. We arrived at the destination, the people got out, and the two guys went at it again right there in the front drive of their apartment complex. I cleared their fare, left rapidly and did no further action.

"I'M SORRY, BUT THAT IS NOT THE 'CHECK ENGINE' LIGHT."

I bought a new Accent in August 2015. It worked just fine for my ride-sharing work for the first six months after that time. Then, the 'check engine' light was lit up around the clock on the dashboard of the car. I was concerned and went to have it looked at by the dealer and by my personal mechanic. Neither location was helpful in this matter even though they told me that there was no harm in leaving the light as is. I decided against any type of repair and continued with the light shining. Almost immediately, numerous passengers called to my attention the fact that I must have an engine problem, since the light was shining.

With this much questioning going on, I decided to create a story that is ninety percent false. From now on, the shining light was not the 'check engine' light at all. It was a light that I had installed in the car dashboard that would serve as a fool-proof test of whether a passenger were sober or not. From that point on, when a passenger exclaimed, "Hey, there must be something wrong with your car. Your engine light is lit up!", my response would be the same. I asked each one if they were sure they were seeing a 'check engine' light. I would tell them, "I'm sorry, but that is not the 'check engine' light. It is my fool-proof test of whether a passenger is sober or drunk. Every sober passenger will exclaim that the engine light is shining. Every drunk passenger will exclaim 'Why are you burning a Christmas ornament?' I submit to you that any drunk passenger will see a Christmas ornament in my RIDESHARE car."

MY WORST FARE EVER

My worst fare 'ever' took place in the downtown area of Austin, about five blocks west of Congress Avenue on Sixth Street. It was around two in the morning. I got a request to pick up someone and drove up to a guy who was waving for me to pull over. He helped a female companion, a very tipsy young lady, into the back seat and then got in beside her. He said we were going to his apartment. I turned left onto West Avenue and crossed Fifth Street and was in an unlit street. There were no street lights working in this area since it was undergoing construction. The man blurted out, "You don't know where you are, do you?" I told him to give me about thirty seconds and I would know perfectly. He retorted, "You are the worst driver I have ever had. Just go to my car a few blocks from here and let us out." He led me the three blocks to his car and he and his lady got out. He left my car with a scowl on his face, shouting out, "You get one star from me." I went one block, cleared the fare and returned the favor of giving him a one star evaluation. I hope he tripped over the curb and fell face down before entering his car, seeing multiple stars as he did so.

THE TALES OF 'MY STUFF'

One late evening I picked up four people from the front of a drinking establishment in the Rainey Street entertainment district. We began the trip to their destination without any problem. I introduced myself and they introduced themselves individually. We got about five blocks down the street and the woman in the middle of the backseat said, "Hey, Mr. Driver. Do you want to see my stuff?" Everyone burst into laughter. I thought about my answer for a few seconds. Before I could answer, the guy in the front seat blurted out, " Don't bother. They are not that great to look at". More laughter followed by a trip full of meaningless chatter. Do you think the guy in the front seat got his butt kicked when he got home?

One late evening there was a similar crowd in my car. The question hits the scene. "Hey Mister Driver, wanna see my stuff? I thought about it as the carload of inebriated passengers laughed and laughed. I came up with a wise crack. I said, "Lady, you have two problems with my taking a peek. First, I am not supposed to take my eyes off of the road while I am driving passengers for this ride-sharing company. Secondly, I have a FOOT FETISH!". Apparently, the woman was not going to be outdone. She took off her shoe from one foot and put the foot on the console between me and the front seat passenger. At the moment that I stopped for a red light. I looked down and commented, " Your paint job is exceptional. I am so sad that I cannot get my toenail paint job to look so good by its holding the paint so well". Everyone gasped and then let out loud howls of laughter. Fetishes win again.

THE 'STINKY' FARE

Every RIDESHARE driver in the whole world must have had at least one passenger(s) riding in their car who reeked with body odor. I had that happen to me during the South By Southwest Festival in Austin in 2016. I had just driven a lady from downtown to her hairdresser at The Domain. She got out of the car. I cleared her fare and immediately got a request for pickup from the hotel around the corner. I drove to the pickup location and four guys got into the car. I set the trip in motion and listened to them chatter in the French language. They told me that this were their first time to attend South By and that they had arrived last night from Paris, France. I asked them where they were going downtown and they told me their destination in English. I made the trip as fast as I could, going south on Loop One in light traffic, after taking a whiff of the scents which they brought with them. They reeked of body odor. Obviously not one of them had brought their cologne bottle with them from their home country, nor did they bother to use the luxurious shower in their fancy hotel room. Perhaps they were accustomed to freshening up by using the bidet, but could not find one in this hotel. I let them out on Trinity Street, cleared their fare, and quickly turned off the driver application. I rolled down all four windows and had to drive around downtown with windows down for the next fifteen minutes for the purpose of clearing the stink from inside my car.

THE LONGEST ETHIOPIAN RIDE

The longest Ethiopian ride I have taken was from a dormitory on the campus of Texas State University in San Marcos to an Ethiopian restaurant in Round Rock, Texas, The trip was about forty-five miles. A young lady got into the back seat of my car. I introduced myself and told her that I lived in San Marcos. She replied by telling me that she was a Graduate Student from Addis Abbaba. I asked why she were traveling so far on this date. She said that she had met another student at the campus who was born in Ethiopia and had immigrated with his family to Round Rock. She said that she had an invitation to dine with the new-found friend at the Ethiopian restaurant which had been started by his family a year ago. I asked her if she was familiar with the foods that were offered at this restaurant and whether the family could find ethnic foods at outlets in the Austin area. She said that she understood that the ethnic foods were very hard to find and that she expected that the meal she ate later today would be very sparse and not taste at all like the meals to which she were accustomed back in her native country. She asked whether I was interested in taking a break when I got to the destination of the restaurant and coming inside to try some of the entrees on the menu. I declined, telling her that I needed to make my quota of fares before getting time for any meal break, no matter how big or meager the meal might be. I want all of my readers to know that one day I will return to Round Rock to look for that restaurant and enjoy some ethnic food.

THE SHORTEST ETHIOPIAN RIDE

One Friday about six in the evening, I got a request to pick up a fare from the JW Hotel on Second Street. Four women of African descent got into the car. They were the tallest women I have ever seen in my whole life. The shortest must have been six feet six inches and the tallest six feet eleven inches. Their heads almost scraped the roof of my car on the inside. They were speaking a language that were foreign to me. I asked them in English to tell me their language and to tell me where they were from. They told me that they were from Ethiopia and were in Austin for the weekend from Houston. One lady told me that they were all attending The University of Houston Graduate School of Business and Finance and needed a break. Someone at their university advised that Austin is the best fun place for them to spend a weekend and to eat good Texas barbecue. Their destination was a barbecue outlet on

Barton Springs Street. Before they got out of the car at their destination, I recommended that they order MARBLED BRISKET. I told them that this was the style of cut on a cooked piece of beef and it would melt in their mouths. So much for tall Ethiopian women wearing four inch heels and searching for good barbeque. The trip from the hotel on Congress Avenue to the barbecue venue on Barton Springs took less than five minutes and I was not allowed enough time to have these nice women put some comments in their native language into the journal which I carry in the car for such occasions.

NEVER ASSUME ANYTHING
- -

I have learned the lesson that it is never correct to assume anything about anything since I have been a driver. I want to illustrate this lesson by telling readers that I recently found SOUL TOWN on my SIRIUS XM car radio. I got excited immediately. I could hardly wait to play this type of music, which features the best musicians with the best soul music ever written and played in America. I was driving near the Outlet Mall in San Marcos, Texas when I made the discovery while parked inside the mall waiting for a fare. I was hoping to get a request from some young people so that I could play soul music and teach them that I had grown up with music as good or better than rap. I got a request for a pickup in less than ten minutes. I drove up to a group of four young people, whom I assumed were African Americans. I was so excited. I was going to have the opportunity to introduce some young people to the famous soul singers of the sixties. They would hear Ella Fitzgerald, Bobby Brown, James Brown, and several other stars of the 'soul' scene as I played channel 49 on SIRIUS XM. They loaded a dozen packages into the trunk of the car and got in, ready to go. Oops. They immediately began speaking with one another in Spanish. The lady in the front seat told me the destination in English. I greeted all of these passengers in Spanish and asked whether they were from Texas. They told me that they were citizens of The Dominican Republic and were in New Braunfels, Texas on a work visa. I decided that I would play the radio very softly and let them talk in their native language. I will never again assume anything about anything.

THE 'COOKIE' RUNS

The 'cookie' runs can happen for a ride-share driver any time of day or night. I have done the runs at all hours of the day and night. One such run took place when I picked up four UT female students from the Sixth Street entertainment district after midnight and was driving them back to West campus. Two of them in the back seat kept yelling that they were starving for food and could not hold out without food until they got back to their dorm. I told them loudly that I had a solution for their hunger problem. I drove down Lavaca Street going north, turned left onto Fifteenth Street, got into the left turn lane and made a turn onto Guadalupe and immediately hung a left into the front drive of a well-known downtown hotel. I did not explain before hand to the passengers that I had befriended most of the valet workers about three months earlier. I just pulled up to the valet stop area, rolled down the front passenger window and said to the valet guy, " I have four starving UT students in my car. Can you help with solving the hunger problem?" The valet guy smiled, turned and walked into the lobby. He returned in less than one minute with hands full of warm, extra-large chocolate chip cookies. He gave two to each of the students and we went on our way. Such is southern hospitality Austin style.

One afternoon on the first day of Spring Break at UT-Austin, I got a request for a pickup from an apartment building on Guadalupe Street. A young lady was waiting and had two large pieces of luggage beside her. I loaded the luggage into the trunk of the car and asked her to get into the car. She said that she was on her way to the airport. I asked her for the time of her flight and her flight destination. She said that she was meeting a girlfriend for a flight to London, England which was leaving in about an hour. I asked if she had a snack packed for her flight since I had been on an overseas flight myself a time or two. She said that she barely had time for packing and did not pack a snack. I told her that she could not go on such a long flight without a snack. I drove south on Guadalupe until I came to the front drive of that well-known hotel, drove up to valet and rolled down the front passenger window, asking the valet guy for cookies for a snack for the lady in the car with me. I told him that he may prevent her starvation by offering her cookies. He went into the lobby and returned in less than thirty-seconds with two warm chocolate chip cookies. She accepted them, put them into her purse and we continued towards the airport to catch the flight. I told her when we arrived at the airport that it may be a good idea to share the cookies so as to avoid a fight with her travel companion.

THE SAGA OF THE DRUNK FRESHMEN GIRLS

So you think College freshmen girls are hilarious when they are stone-cold sober. Think how they are when not sober. I have a good one for you about this. Late one Saturday night, after the midnight hour, I was driving around the Square in downtown San Marcos. I got a request to do a pick up about fourteen minutes away. I took off from the Square and followed the app directions down Post Road, then Lime Kiln Road and then a left turn onto Hilliard Road. I drove about three miles and the app showed that the passenger(s) stop was on the right. There was a guy on the side of the road moving a lit flashlight around in circles. He guided me to the shoulder, walked up to me and asked me to pull up about twenty feet. He asked me to tell him the name of the rider. I told him and he walked off into the darkness of the night, returning with four staggering young women. Obviously, they were college students and very badly in need of a ride. They got into the car and I asked for their destination. One blurted out loudly, "This will not be an easy trip. We each live in a different dorm. Plus, we are starving. We first want to go to McDonald's for some food. Then, we need to go to our dorms. As we drove towards town, the girls got into a fierce argument about who was paying for the food and whether they should go inside to place the order or go through the drive-up. One girl kept screaming that it was her decision to make, since the ride-share bill was on her credit card. Once that matter got settled, I managed to get in a word. I asked how long they had been in San Marcos and attending our wonderful University. They screamed at once, "We are all Freshmen!!!" I thought to myself that this would be a hefty challenge. It was imperative that I get these overgrown children to their destinations in safe condition. That would please both me and their parents to no end. Besides, I am totally dedicated to driving late at night for the sole purpose of protecting members of the next GREAT generation. We pulled into the parking lot of McDonald's and all four girls got out and staggered to the door of the establishment. They seemed to be having a shoving match with one another as they waited in line to place orders and get their yummies. Finally, they came out to the car and we resumed our trip to the designated dorms. To my surprise, these were young ladies who were serious about Sunday church attendance. One girl got out at each stop, put her head back inside the car and screamed, "I'll see ya'll in church about eleven this morning". I had no recourse at each stop but to comment in a calm but assuring voice, "Young lady, after tonight you need to be in church". Funny thing. Each of the young ladies thought that comment was hilarious.

HOW SMALL IS THE WORLD

One Saturday evening, I was driving in Austin and became very hungry. I decided to invite my nephew, Daniel, who is also a RIDESHARE driver, to join me for some good barbeque. I told him to take a break from driving and meet me at 7:30 pm at the new barbeque place on Barton Springs Drive. We met outside and went in to get a place in line. Two young ladies came to the line and stood beside us. They were talking about all there was to offer on the menu and obviously were at this establishment for the first time. They said that everything on the menu looked fabulous and then asked me to recommend a good choice. I told them to ask for marbled brisket with all of the trimmings. Daniel and I placed our orders and went to the drink dispenser to get our drinks. I turned to see where we might sit and saw that there was only one table unoccupied in the whole place. I walked back to the food line and told the two ladies that they were welcome to sit with us since only one table were vacant. Daniel and I sat down and in a few minutes the two young ladies joined us. I started a conversation with my usual friendliness. I asked where the two were from. One lady said that she grew up in Austin but went away to college. Her friend was on her first visit from the east, where she and her companion were close college friends. I asked the Austin lady if her parents were still in Austin. She told me that her parents were attached to The University of Texas at Austin in The College of Architecture. I responded, "Then they must certainly know my good friend, Lizzy Dee, who is a shinning star in that Department." They young lady began to laugh almost uncontrollably. She nearly screamed, "Lizzy Dee is my Mother!" Then, I remembered that I had met this young lady when she was about four years old. I told her so and then asked about her grandfather, Leon. She told me that he had reached ninety years of age and lived next door to her parents. I told her to give him my very best and to remind him that he was the architect on the design of the first residence I had built for myself in the area.

THE IRISHMAN AND OTHER DIGNITARIES

I have had the good fortune of being the Rideshare driver for several dignitaries in my three years' experience. Let me tell you about a few that are definitely memorable.

I once picked up a well-dressed gentleman who was making a trip from north Austin to a fashionable restaurant to the south some ten miles. He spoke in a very thick brogue, one which I had not heard since Rose and I were on our honeymoon in Ireland. I introduced myself and asked his name. He told me that his name is Kevin O. I asked if he were visiting Austin from another country. He replied that he was here for a few months from the City of Dublin, Ireland. I was very excited to hear that he came to Austin from Ireland. I had not had a conversation in years with anyone who lived in Dublin. It was back in 1983, the year of my marriage, that Rose and I visited Dublin during a five-day stay in Ireland. I told the gentleman that my wife and I both have fond memories of Ireland. My best memory was my trying to drive the rental car and make my way around the city. It was terribly difficult since it seemed at the time that the name of every street changed every six to ten blocks. He laughed and stated that the situation is still very much the same. I told him also that my wife was of Irish extraction and that her grandparents Burke had immigrated from a small village in the shadows of Dublin. He replied that probably that were so, since so many people living in Dublin had the last name of Burke. I then told him that Austin was a great vacation destination for anyone from any other place in the world. He said that his trip was primarily business-related. I asked, "How so?" He told me that he had been sent to Austin to establish an Irish Consulate here. I was really impressed and I told him so. He said that many companies in Dublin had offices in Austin, Texas and that his services were badly needed.

Six weeks went by. I was at home one morning drinking my usual cup of coffee and reading the Austin Statesman. On the front page of Metro/State, I see a headline, "Irish President visits Austin." I see that the article shows a photo of a ribbon-cutting ceremony. The news article talked about how important the Irish Consulate of Austin would be to the local business community and how proud Austin was because it was host to a consulate. The photo above the article showed The President of Ireland was sharing the chore of cutting a ribbon with my new acquaintance, Kevin O.

Two weeks later, I got a request for pickup on a corner on Congress in downtown Austin. Two men and a woman got into the car. One man and the lady were speaking English with a heavy Irish brogue. I was so excited. I had no doubt that they were tourists. I excitedly told them that their home country has an official representation in Austin, Texas. I told them the story about Kevin O. They responded that they had just come from his office. It seems that the lady tourist had encountered a problem with her passport and that Kevin O. was able to rapidly resolve her issue.

Six months later, I had a request for pick up at Austin-Bergstrom International Airport. I drive up to 'Arrivals' and picked up a gentleman from pillar J. He was carrying a large bag of golf clubs which would not fit into the trunk or back seat of my car. He and I lowered the back seat and he put the clubs into the trunk. This was the first time in over two thousand five-hundred trips that I found the need to lower the back seat in order to accommodate a passenger and their luggage. The gentleman got into the car and requested that he be taken to his home in Lakeway. This gentleman was speaking in a heavy Irish brogue. I was so excited to find another person from Ireland in the grand city of Austin. The trip was long, so we had time for some good conversation. The passenger asked me to tell him some of my best stories about driving RIDESHARE. I began with my story about Kevin O. To my delight and surprise, this passenger revealed that he knows Kevin O. He told me that he has been employed for many years with the Dell Corporation and had assisted with the formation of the company branches in his home country of Ireland. He told me that Kevin O. has been very helpful to him in his personal and professional dealings since the opening of the Irish Consulate in Austin.

It is so interesting that some of my stories, especially this one, are totally circular. I hope to find more stories which are the same as this one in the years to come as I continue to drive in the Austin region.

The City of San Marcos presents eight Thursday night events of free music for its citizens during the summer months. Often these events are a source of numerous RIDESHARE trips. The events are so well-attended that most people find it difficult to find adequate parking nearby and need a ride for their ice chests full of drinks, their wives and children and their lawn chairs. I have transported people to and from the event for the past three summers. Then too, there are the same people who need a ride home or to a car that is parked at a great distance from the event. On one evening, I met a gentleman, his wife and his two daughters after the event who were in need of a ride to their home in San Antonio. The gentleman sat in the front seat and we began to chat. He shared that he was the manager for four hispanic bands that had won multiple grammy awards. He was in San Marcos this evening because one of his bands,'Los Texmaniacs' was doing the program in the park. I told him of my involvement in the community of San Marcos and he was happy to know that there were so many happenings in this area of Texas. He told me that his name is J. Garza and that he and his bands would be happy to participate in fund-raising events in the future to help non-profits to gather the resources they need to serve the public. I think that it was a stroke of good luck for me to drive in San Marcos on that Thursday night and to have met a person of such notoriety.

THE STARS COME OUT AT NIGHT

It is a busy Saturday night in Austin. I get a request for a ride from an apartment complex near the UT campus. I arrive and an oversized athletic-looking man gets into the passenger side back seat. He was so tall that his head almost touched the roof of the interior of my little car. I introduced myself and asked whether he was a football player. He said that he was, but during the off-season he had a job at an establishment in the Domain. That establishment was his destination. I then asked what position he played. He told me that he was an offensive tight end on the UT varsity team. I said, "That must mean that you get to catch a few passes in every game". He confirmed that and he added that he was the guy who caught the winning touchdown pass the last time UT beat OU in Dallas. Wow! I was giving a ride to Cal. I asked for his autograph and he gave it to me willingly. This was one of my good fortune trips in Austin during 2016.

Here it is, a rain-soaked Monday in May 2017. I get a call to Jester Dormitory. Two guys come racing through the storm and jump into the car. Between the two of them, they carried a weight of over 700 pounds. I asked whether they were football players. They said that they were, so I asked whether they knew Cal. They said that indeed they did and that he had just signed a contract with the Jaguars. They then told me that they were going into their sophomore year at UT and expected to make the starting offensive line, one as the right guard and the other as the right tackle. I asked them to please give me their autograph. They did so willingly. I was able afterward to read the autograph of one of them. It was Imade. I recalled that two years ago he was near the top of the list of the Fabulous Fifty high school recruits in Texas. I could not read the name of the other player, so I will have to see who is playing right offensive guard in the 2017 season to find the identity of my second passenger.

THE BIGGEST TIP TRIP

My biggest tip trip was the one from a well-known bar on IH35 north, near the city limits of Pflugerville, Texas. I was called to pick up a fare by two women about one-thirty in the morning. I took them to their residence in the Travis Heights area, turned off the app, and headed for an early breakfast at IHOP. I was getting out of my car in the IHOP parking lot when my phone rang. It was one of the two women from the last fare giving me a call. She was frantic. She thinks she left her expensive cell phone in my car. I looked back, saw it, and asked her how to return it. She gave me her address and I went to her home at once. I drove up and she was waiting for me curbside. I handed her the phone and she thanked me profusely. She told me that she and her friend had spent all of their cash money at the bar, but she had found a one hundred dollar bill in her chest-of-drawers after she called me. She told me she had been saving it, since it had gotten washed in her washing machine. She told me that, even though it had been thoroughly washed and was very pale, that it may still be good. I took it to my bank on Monday morning, where I was told that they could not cash it. My banker gave me the website to which I could go in order to find out how to exchange the bill. I did so the same morning. I mailed the tarnished bill to the appropriate agency and within two weeks I received a government check in the amount of $94.65 Whoopie!!!

COMMENTS THAT I ALWAYS WANTED TO RECEIVE

"Charles was fantastic".
June, 2017

"What a great trip! Charlie rocks!"
June, 2017

"Thanks for the recommendations, Charlie".
June, 2017

"Great guy. God bless him".
April, 2017

"Best man to talk to. Thanks".
February, 2017

"He's the sweetest older gentleman I've met. Very kind and gets to the destination quick. Loved this ride.
February, 2017

"You're a great man. Thank you for all you have done for our community and thank you for getting me home safe".
January, 2017

"Charlie is such a sweetheart. Not only does he listen to good ole classic country tunes, but he went out of his way to take care of his passengers. Thanks for the southern hospitality, Charlie".
June, 2016

"Charles is the best. So kind and friendly".
March, 2016

"Such a pleasant ride. Very sweet man. Would recommend 10/10".
January, 2016

"What a beautiful soul. So gentle with the kids. Plus, candy! Uplifted my whole day".
October, 2016

"Great conversation. Clean vehicle. Very nice person".
August, 2015

"He was the best ride-sharing driver ever! So informative and knowledgeable of Austin. Made our drive so wonderful! We can only hope to get him again".
July, 2015

"Charlie is awesome. Told me all the must-do places in Austin. He obviously loves his city and his job. Great driver!".
July, 2015

"If visiting, ask him places to see. This guy knows everything".
April, 2015

"The best Austin tour guide. Also, his wife made Easter treats for us".
April, 2015

"One of my best drivers ever. Very friendly. Accepting of my guide dog and very nice to have as a driver".
January, 2015

"Charlie is the most helpful and friendly driver I've ever had the privilege of riding with".
September, 2014

"He made a regular ride-sharing ride a great experience".
July, 2017

"Charlie, you are a very likeable person and one of the nicest drivers I've had living in Austin. I wish you the best.' J from Austin.
July, 2016

"So much love for this little moment!" mcordivin.
July 2017

"Hey, Charlie! I love your positivity and friendliness. Stay humble. Stay kind. Thanks for taking us to Float Fest. You were great".
July, 2017

"Never give up on anything in life. Whether it is love or yourself. You keep on going! Smile and enjoy what life has to offer. Madi, July, 2017

"It's seven am and I'm hung over. Charlie's talking is keeping me from thinking how badly I want to throw up. So, Charlie, thanks for that. Thanks for talking up a storm. I appreciate your being here when a semi-drunk/hung-over girl needs to get home". July, 2017

"Thanks for the ride, Charlie. You were super friendly and made my ride back to the airport very enjoyable. Stay positive!" Bari, July, 2017

"Charlie! Thank you for the awesome ride. It was great to hear about Austin from a local. Our ride back to the airport(Portland bound) was very entertaining and finished off our trip right!"
Tarek and Jaime, July, 2017

"Charlie, you're the man. Love meeting new people through RIDESHARE. You're one of a kind. God Bless!" Heather, July, 2017

"Hello. I'm Kadija, from Toronto, Canada. In town for the American Association of University Presses. Austin is awesome" July, 2017

"It is just amazing that most ride-share drivers in this area are in their 20s and 30s. Then, we see Charlie driving in the hurricane rains and he is is his 50s." Fernando Murra, owner, Nichols Tire and Automotive. September, 2017 This is my favorite quote all-time. This is wonderful. My real birthday is September 26, 1941.

"This was my first ride experience. Charlie was an angel. He rescued me from having to stay in Tanger Outlets with my two daughters any longer today. He was very, very courteous and respectful!" September, 2017

THE FORT HOOD TRIP-A CLEAN SLEEP

Here it is. A Sunday night arrives. I get a request for a trip around eight-thirty p.m. from the Kyle, Texas area. I drive from San Marcos,

Texas into a residential area just south of Kyle. Four young men walk to my car, each carrying a large duffle bag. The fellow who gets into the front seat tells me that they are traveling back to Ft. Hood, Texas. That destination is ninety miles to the north of here. I begin the drive and strike up a conversation with the guy in the front seat. He lets me know that he and his buddies just finished Army boot camp and had the weekend off. He invited seven of his graduate buddies to come to his home in Kyle for the weekend and that the other four guys just left in another RIDESHARE car. He tells me that they all played very hard for the past two days and they were going back to Killeen, Texas and Ft. Hood to begin their first assignments. I suggested that since it were so late in the evening we were going to encounter a bottleneck of traffic near downtown Austin. I told the guy in front that it would be quicker and safer for us to use the toll road. He concurred and we entered the toll lane at Buda, Texas. Almost immediately I could hear snoring coming from the backseat. I could see two of the soldiers using headphones and hear a light sound of rap music. Ten minutes later, I hear snoring from the front. Good golly. All four of my passengers were sleeping soundly. So, I would have to continue in total silence. I had never heard such loud snoring and deep inhaling coming from anyone. There was never before anything like this. No one stirred until we stopped at the front gate of Ft. Hood and the security guard looked into my car and asked what was our business tonight. The guys woke up immediately, got out of the car, showed identification, grabbed their duffle bags and walked through the main gate, never to be seen again. I was a bit worried about the condition of the interior of my car. I pulled to the side of the road under a large street lamp and got out to check the front and back of my car, looking to see if the floor boards were full of sawdust caused by all of the snoring. Nothing there. I had encountered a clean SLEEP and nothing more. I gladly got back onto the highway and began my trek home, $99.00 dollars wealthier.

MY FIRST DETOX TRIP

My first detox trip was in April 2017. I got a request for pickup from Austin to go out to Dripping Springs. There was a terrible downpour and a ferocious lightening storm. I was a bit concerned since it was already eleven at night. I drove and drove down U.S. Highway 290 West, through Oak Hill, past the county line and Belterra, through the town area of Dripping Springs until five miles later I got the command to "turn right here". I met a middle-aged woman who met me in her car. She asked me to give a ride to her friend, who was in the front seat. Her passenger needed a ride to a detox center to enable her to attend to her drinking problem. This was my first time to give someone a ride to a detox location, but I figured out why just as I took one deep breath. The passenger went on and on about how she was not going to check in unless this were a program that promised to last only five days. We continued to Dripping Springs, went right at the stop light at RR12. We turned left onto FM150 towards Driftwood, made a left onto FM1826 and continued past The Salt Lick. We turned right onto the road to Buda and I began to worry since I had never seen any sign of any business between this point and downtown Buda. The app guided me a bit further and then directed me to turn into a dimly-lit entrance to a property. There was a gate phone to my left so I called on it and a lady told me she would open the gate immediately. We drove into the property with the passenger yelling at me that she had been hoodwinked into coming to this location. At once we saw an attendant. I shouted out the window that I was bringing a lady for help. The attendant gave me the high sign and I drove further, stopping at the front steps to the first building. The woman got out, holding her little travel bag and cursing under her alcoholic breath, "This had better be my kind of place". I backed up ten feet, did a u-turn and hooked 'em for Austin. Whew, what an experience!

THE HONEYMOON TRIP

It is ten-thirty at night on Saturday. I had gotten a request for pickup earlier in the week on my app. It was out on Fitzhugh Road in Hays County. I accepted the request with the intention that this would be my final trip of the night. I supposed some young dudes were tanked up on alcohol and were in need of a safe ride home. I met minimal traffic all the way down the highway and turned right onto the part of Fitzhugh Road that is in Travis County. I had not been on this part of the road in the last five years. My trip was pleasant. I continued to negotiate all of the hairpin turns and curves on this part of Fitzhugh and eventually came to the intersection with Ranch Road 12 North. I continued on. The road got darker. No street lights and no homes with lights on. This reminded me of the roads at night in the northern part of Minnesota. I used my trusty flashlight for the next five miles, stopping at every other mail box to check the address. Finally, I arrived at the pickup location and took a left turn and went down a long drive. As I approached, I heard loud music. I got to a well-lit area and realized that this was bigger than I expected. There was designated parking and a huge barn-like structure. I hit the app on the word 'arrived' and no one came out for about two minutes. Then, I realized that this was the party after a wedding and that people were forming a line towards my car from the front door of the barn. I kept looking intently. I see the bride and groom coming through the line as the people toss rice and shout loudly. One guy in the line ran to the passenger side back door of my car, opened it and said, "It will be just a minute". The minute went by and, to my surprise, the bride and groom head for my car. They get into the back seat still dressed in wedding regalia. The bride proclaims loudly, "Let's get out of here! You are taking us to our honeymoon bungalow!" This was so much fun that I joined in also. I drove away rapidly with my right hand pressed firmly on the car horn for the next half-mile. The trip to the bungalow was a fare of eight dollars for me, plus the twenty dollar tip from the bride. More people should use RIDESHARE as a getaway car from their wedding celebration. It is safe and rapid.

TRIPS TO THE EMERGENCY ROOM

Those of us who are drivers sometimes have the chore of assisting college students to get medical attention for one type of problem or other. They seem always to be short of money for big emergencies. I am clearly understanding of that predicament since I did not have a regular stash of cash on a monthly basis during my months of attending college.

One afternoon I was driving away from The Yellow Store, at which I had just filled my gas tank for a bargain price. I immediately got a request for pickup from an apartment complex at the far end of Mill Street across town in San Marcos. I had no reason to think otherwise than that this were a request from a student who had missed the bus to classes. I got to the complex and notified the person who had made the request for the ride. A young lady of student age came out and got into the car. It was the middle of the day on a weekday and I expected that she would be carrying a bag of books. No books! No bag! The young lady was inhaling and exhaling excessively. She said, "Get me to the hospital emergency room as quickly as possible. I am having a reaction to a medication I just took a few minutes ago". I was a bit concerned, to say the least. She was not doing well and I supposed that she was not able to afford the trip to the hospital by ambulance. I did keep asking her whether I needed to pull over and make a call to EMS for her. She told me, "Please, don't do that? I am almost flat broke. Besides, this happens at least twice every semester". I raced to West Sessom Street, turned left on Aquarena Springs and then I turned onto the IH35 south access road, veered left and flew onto IH35 already moving about seventy-five miles per hour. At this rate of speed, we would arrive at the hospital within less than four minutes. I kept checking the rear view mirror to get a quick glimpse of my passenger and to assess if she were alert enough to make it safely to Central Texas Medical Center. I tried to keep her conscious by asking over and over, "Are you sure we do not need to call EMS, pull over and wait for them to arrive?" She begged that I continue on, so I hit the gas peddle even more and we were going about eighty-five when I approached the overpass at Seguin Highway exit. I began braking, moved right and immediately realized that the road was going to be clear as I moved down the access road towards the light at Wonder World Drive. I approached the turn and got a green light. I made a left turn and gunned the engine, surging towards the final traffic light before the hospital driveway. I made the left at the hospital parking lot, hooked a right and drove up to the 'arrival' door, stopping abruptly. The young lady jumped out of the car and ran to the door, never again to be seen. I have the impression that RIDESHARE saved the day and a small stash of college money for this student.

THE TACO STORIES

The Taco Stories came from my intense desire to take part fully in the festivities of the 2016 Presidential Election last November. This story is funny to Democrats and to Republicans, depending on how I tell it. Here we go. This is the story of the first time I took my great-granddaughter, Daisy Juanita, for tacos at 'THE TACO PLACE'. I told the story one way or the other, depending on how my passengers answered the question of whether they support Democrats or Republicans.

"My friends", I would begin," I want to tell you about the first trip I made to a nice taco establishment here in Austin with my great granddaughter, Daisy Juanita. I tell it one way or another, if you prefer to support either the Democrat or the Republican during the November presidential election." Here goes, for better or for worse:

I took Daisy inside for a taco or two. I told her that there were two very delicious tacos on the menu and that she could make a choice of which one to try on her first visit. I told her about the contents of 'The Democrat' and the contents of 'The Republican'. Once I told her, she said that it was clear that 'The Republican' was a barbeque taco and that it were late enough in the day for barbecue." She said, "Pawpaw, I want 'The Republican'"(Democrat). I ordered the taco right away. The waitress brought it to the table, set it in front of Daisy and she unwrapped it hurriedly. She bit into it, made a terrible face and proclaimed, "Yuk, Pawpaw! This is awful", as she spit it onto her plate. Like a good clean freak, I took her napkin, wiped up "The Republican"(Democrat), and tossed it into the trash bin where it belonged.

'THE RIDESHARE MOVE TO CANADA' STORY/2016 PRESIDENTIAL RACE

I never intend to accept a passenger who want me to drive all the way to Canada. However, I did receive an interesting email from a ride-sharing company about six weeks before the November 2016 Presidential election. The email stated that should a certain Presidential candidate for presidency of The United States of America be elected, this ride-sharing company was going to uproot and move to Canada. As a final farewell to drivers, the company intended to send each driver a certified check in the amount of two thousand dollars. There would be one stipulation. The driver had to use the money exclusively to pay tuition to take classes at a job training facility on how to properly lay bricks. Story over!!! (I do hope readers get the gist and inuendo of this story). I want everyone to know that I look every morning in the mail box at the front of my residence. It has been months since the presidential election and the check has yet to arrive. So, I carry on about thirty hours weekly as a part-time RIDESHARE driver.

A VERY SHORT HALF-DAY TRIP

It is the second day of South By Southwest in 2015. I am driving near the airport and I get a request for a ride from the arrival site at the airport. I see my passenger waving his hand at me from the pillar marked G. I pull to the curb and he gets in. He tells me that he wants to go to a hotel in the downtown area. We drive there quickly but he reveals that he is here from Los Angeles for the purpose of being a representative of his nationwide company during the festivities this week. I stop in the front of his hotel. He unloads his gear and I go on my way.

I am driving the next day just after noon. I get a request for a pickup at the intersection of Fourth Street and San Jacinto. I arrive and I see that it is the man from Los Angeles. He is accompanied by a young lady. They get into the back seat of my car and he tells me that the young lady is a co-worker, but her office is in Orlando. He tells me that he has searched "Google" for a good swimming hole and he has decided that he and his friend should go to Hamilton Pool. I asked whether he knew how far away that destination happened to be. He said he did not care how far. It just looked like the place to be.

We went on our way. I got onto Loop One south and curved onto 290 west, towards Dripping Springs. Ten miles down, I made a right turn onto Fitzhugh Road. We continued some ten miles until I made a right turn onto RR12 north. We eventually came to Hamilton Pool Road, with another seven miles to go. I saw the sign for Reimers Ranch Park and turned into the drive. About one hundred yards down, there was a woman selling entry tickets. She tells us that the park and pool will be open for another two and a half hours. Then, she warns that there is no cell phone connectivity in this area of Hays County because of the peaks and valleys. My male passenger begs of me, "Charlie, please let us get out here. Then, come back and pick us up at five pm just at closing time. I will make it worth your time". I did not hesitate to say that I would help him since my part of the fare one way was a whopping fifty-five dollars. The couple got out of the car and I drove off, eventually stopping in Dripping Springs at my favorite eatery. I had a nice meal, chatted with friends from my local Rotary Club, read part of the daily paper, and then started back to the Park and swimming hole. My passengers came up the hill after I had waited about ten minutes. They requested their ride and I accepted since I were the driver nearest to them. Luckily, they had requested a ride with Rideshare Pool. I got onto Fitzhugh Road for the return trip when I got a request to do a pickup along the way back into Austin. The app directed me back to Dripping Springs, onto US 290 west, with a turn into the Belterra subdivision. We stopped in the subdivision for a woman who was going to the entertainment district on Rainey Street. I continued what turned out to be my longest 'pool' trip so far. We went down Mopac Expressway, exited at Fifth Street and then took a right turn onto San Jacinto. I let the couple off at the front of their hotel. The male passenger handed me a large bill in cash, saying that he was going to pay for my supper. I then went to the Rainey Street area to let off the second female customer. She shared that she had moved here from Moscow and was meeting business associates for an evening of dining and drinking. RIDESHARE would later return her home safely. This entire episode took about five hours and my payoff was over one hundred and forty dollars. This was an easy and rather short time span since I had to drive for only fifty percent of the time that expired.

THE LANDING PAD TRIP

Early on in my days as an RIDESHARE driver, I got a request for pickup at a an apartment complex near the UT west campus in Austin.

I drove up to the front of the complex and a young lady came out and got into the back seat of my car. She was carrying a very small bag with her. I introduced myself and she did likewise. I then asked for her destination. She told me that she was going to the landing pad. The only landing pad it could be was the one used by private planes that landed on the grounds of ABIA. It was also where my stepson had worked parttime doing maintenance work in the evenings. I asked her how far she was traveling today. She replied that she were merely going to work. I thought maybe she was an office worker at the hangar area beside the private planes parked just to the east of the main entrance to ABIA. I was totally wrong. The app directed me towards the airport. As I continued towards the destination, I continued my conversation with this lady passenger. I asked how long she had been working at the airport. She replied that she did not and had never worked at the airport. She told me that she was a dancer at the gentlemen's club named 'The Landing Pad', which was one mile from the entrance to ABIA. She was going to work. I asked if she had been in Austin long. She told me that she grew up here. Last week she had a spat with her Father and he told her to move out. She was using her cell phone at the dinner table and her Father demanded that she turn off the phone for the meal. She refused, got up from the table and went to pack her things. She said that I had picked her up at her new apartment. I asked whether she made good money as a dancer. She told me that most of her money went to pay her tuition at Austin Community College and, starting last week, for her housing and other expenses. She said that the workplace cost her $30.00 per hour to use the venue. Wow! The cost of inflation has truly risen. I thought I had it bad because I was paying RIDESHARE a much smaller weekly rent fee for the use of the phone with the company app. Such is life for dancers and drivers. I left the young lady at the entrance to the club, telling her, "I hope you succeed at the college and become successful in your endeavor."

MY FIRST ACT OF CHIVALRY/HELPING LAURINE

Here I am on my first Sunday to drive in Austin. Business is rather slow as I head over to the area of East Riverside and Wickersham to park in the lot beside the Shell station. I wait about ten minutes before I get a request for pickup at the nearby HEB grocery store. I drive into the parking lot of the store and I see a very short woman standing out front with a basket full of sacks with foodstuff. I got out of the car and helped her to load the sacks into the trunk of my car. I introduce myself and she does likewise. Her name is Laurine. She says that she is from San Salvador, El Salvador and is in Austin to attend English classes at Austin Community College. As we near her apartment complex, I ask which floor of the complex is her floor and who is going to unload the sacks. She tells me that she lives on the third floor and that she has no one to help with unloading. I thought to myself, "Here is a chance for me to do my good deed of the day." I tell her that I would not hear of her lugging these heavy sacks up three flights of stairs on multiple trips. I told her to take one sack upstairs and to open the door of her apartment. I will follow with two more sacks and then return to my car for the last two. She agrees to the plan and we go about the chore. The tasks were completed and I left, supposing that this were the last time I would see Laura. How wrong I was on this score. It was six weeks later when I was working on a Saturday afternoon. Near five pm I got a request for pickup at the same apartment complex and same building at which I had left Laura. I gave notice of arrival and, to my delight, it were Laura. She got into the car and told me that she was headed to the west campus of UT-Austin where she was going to meet a friend. We went on our way and in twenty minutes we were at the front of a dorm building. Laurine asked me to wait while she went into the dorm to get her friend. She went inside and soon returned with a handsome young man behind her. The fellow told me that their destination now was to a new seafood place on the east side of the city. We took off and got to the new restaurant in fifteen minutes. The couple got out at the destination and I told Laurine that it was nice seeing her again and perhaps I would give her a ride one more time or two before she finished her courses.

That was to be the case. One month later, I am again parked in the lot by the Shell Station on Wickersham on a Sunday afternoon. I get a request for pickup and immediately recognize that I was getting another request from Laurine. I give notice of arrival and Laurine comes to the car wearing a very expensive-looking outfit. She tells me that she is again headed to west campus to the dorm of her friend. I make the drive, leave her off at a previous location and drive away to catch another fare. I drove three blocks and I get a request to pickup at the front door of the dorm at which I had left Lauraine I stop, give notice of arrival, and see the same couple come out the door of the dorm building. For this trip, the male friend is wearing a nice sport coat and fancy tie. We take off and we share some pleasantries as I drive to the assigned destination. I find that I am taking this dashing couple to one of the finest new restaurants in the city. I drive up to the valet station, roll down the window on the front passenger side, and tell the valet, "Take care of these people. They are very important people." I drive off and look for another fare full of satisfaction that I may have participated in the birth of a budding romance between two nice young people.

THE WHATABURGER INCIDENT

You all must certainly be aware of the fact that Rideshare drivers sometimes get very hungry once we are in the middle part of a long day of driving people around. This is so true of me. I have to take a food break and have become accustomed to making my stop at the Whataburger outlet at South First Street and Barton Springs Drive. I go there regularly and have good fortune from stopping for a double meat cheese bacon burger, fries and a forty-four ounce Dr. Pepper.

This was the case one Friday afternoon when I was having a lull in business. I had not received a request for pickup in over one and a half hours. I headed for the eatery, went in and ordered my usual and sat and ate once it arrived. I noticed that a man who was dressed in a shabby way came in. He ordered only a cup of coffee and sat down to enjoy it. He looked very haggard and had a forlorn look on his face. I really felt for the guy. I have been without for an hour and a half and he obviously has been doing without since almost the start of time. I decided that I needed to do something to make his day better. I finished my meal, got up and walked up to the counter to speak to the lady who had taken my order today. I asked her to tell me about the guy who had bought the cup of coffee. She told me that he came in every day and sat and drank cups of coffee for hours. I told her that I wanted to pay for a meal for him. I ordered the same items on the menu which comprise my usual meal. I paid for the meal and asked the lady to serve it to the fellow after I had left the eatery. I told her to please tell him this: "This meal was paid for by a customer whose horses came in!" I left the restaurant and returned to the car. I turned on the Rideshare app and within five minutes I got a request for pickup. The extra meal for the guy who was apparently homeless cost me $11.99. The fare I got when I returned to the car brought me $25.00. My life as a Rideshare driver has been filled with incidents like this. When I make an effort to help or to give, I get rewarded double.

MY SHORTEST FARE

My shortest fare was for a couple whom I picked up in a neighborhood off of Parker Street and east Riverside Drive. I picked up the couple, introduced myself and asked where they were from. They said they had just moved to Austin from New York City. I asked what brought them to Austin and the guy blurts out, "I do not like where this is going. Just pull over at the next intersection and let us out". I honored his request. I stopped beside a vacant lot on a seldom used street. They opened the door and got out. I had driven them a distance of four blocks and received the base fare for a trip. I wonder how long they waited at that location for another foolish RIDESHARE driver. It had better not be a driver who is hospitable.

MY SHORTEST CONVERSATION

One weekday afternoon I was driving in downtown San Marcos. I got a pickup request from the middle of the Texas State campus. I went to the pickup location and a female student go into the back seat of the car. I introduced myself and she responded, "I am sorry. I will not tell you my name. I never discuss personal matters." The trip continued to the finish without one word of conversation after that remark from the passenger.

THERE ARE NO 'BUCKEYES' IN LOOZIANNA

I got a request for pickup one weekday evening from the City of New Braunfels. I was still in San Marcos, so the trip to the passengers location took about fifteen minutes in the southbound traffic on IH35. I drove to the front of a nice motel just off of the highway and picked up two anglo young men who told me they were in Texas for the next six weeks doing a construction job. I asked where they lived and they told me that they were living in Houma, Louisiana. They did sound as though they were from southern Louisiana. They told me 'Loozianna' when they said their home state. One of them said, "Weeze just a coupla coonasses that done got some educatin in the vocashanal area of work. So, we been sent here to do the job crekly". I chuckled as I continued to drive towards the assigned destination. Their accents were hilarious to me. I turned onto the access road to IH35 going north when one guy said, "Looka thea, they got a Buckeye gas station". We ain't got nuthin' like that in Houma or any place else in suthun Loozianna". They continued talking about the gasoline station as we moved on north. They suggested that they should one day have enough money to open a Buckeye gas station in Houma, with fifty to sixty pumps just like the Buckeye's in New Braunfels. We arrived at the passengers' destination and before they got out of my car I said that I was giving them my personal cell phone number. They were to call me immediately when they were ready to open the site of the first ever 'Buckeyes' in Louisiana.

KAHLID'S RIDES TO TOWN

I met Kahlid in San Marcos, Texas in November, 2014. He was a student at Texas State. He gave me a request for pickup one weekday afternoon and said that he would have to make multiple stops and then return to his apartment. He shared that he was an international student and was in an undergraduate program. He said that he and his brother were both enrolled in a college in Texas, but were reared in countries that were ruled by an emir. His parents now lived in Quatar. He was a citizen because he was born when his Mother attended a university in New York. The country from which he came to Texas was the third one that was ruled by a person with that title. Our first stop was at a bank machine near downtown. Next we went to the local grocery store, where Kahlid bought some cleaning supplies. The third stop was at a hamburger joint on the access of IH35. Kahlid told me that this would be a lengthy stop since he could see that there was a line of people ordering food. He was gone about ten minutes. He returned with a huge fountain drink in one hand and a large paper sack in the other. I asked him what he had ordered and he said that he was accustomed to getting a large bacon-cheese burger at each visit as well as a large order of french fries and a sweet item for dessert. I drove Kahlid back to his apartment and supposed that I would not see him again for a long time. How wrong I was. He used my car four more times during the next two months. He did the same multiple stops, but twice added one more stop for office supplies or computer ware. At the end of the sixth time that Kahlid used my RIDESHARE car, I asked him why it were that he always bought a burger for his meal. He responded by telling me that he had no choice because he never learned to cook. I told him immediately that the next time I had to take him to order a burger that I would instead head my car to the local grocery market, buy nutritious food, and take him directly to my home where my wife and I would teach him how to cook a decent meal. He unloaded his booty and headed for his apartment door. I thought that was the last I would see of Khalid.

KHALID'S TRIP TO ASIA

My very next encounter with Khalid was when he called me on my cell phone. I was at home taking a break and my driver app were turned off. Indeed I was wrong about never seeing him again. It is a Tuesday afternoon and I told him that I would not be driving this evening. He said, "Oh, no, no, no! I am not looking for a ride today. I need a ride to the Austin airport on Saturday morning. It is of the utmost importance that I go to my family. My Mom is demanding that I be with the family during Ramadan. I really must go home. Can you help me?" I told him that I would be able to help him. On Saturday morning, I would arrive at his apartment complex and call him I explained. Then, he could request a RIDESHARE driver. Since I would be the closest driver, I would get the request for pickup. He thanked me and then hung up. He called again on Thursday, in a panic state. He said that he had a major problem with the bank and they would not release the use of his credit card. He is not able to use the card, even to pay for a car ride. "What can I do, Charlie?", he asked. I told him that I would still give him a ride to the airport on Saturday since I planned to drive in Austin all day on that day. I asked that he call to remind me again on Friday night. He gave me a call about nine at night on Friday. I asked whether he had money for his trip. He told me, "Not really. I have thirteen dollars to my name right now." I asked whether that would get him some refreshments in airports along the way. He told me that it would not help because he had to use the thirteen dollars to pay the entry fee into the country when he arrived at his destination. I told him that I would see him in the morning and that I could help with a few dollars for his trip. I got up early, went to town and got to my bank at opening time. I went to my line of credit, withdrew two one hundred dollar bills and sealed it in a bank envelope. I drove to the apartment complex, called Khalid and waited for him to come down to the car. He came down in a few minutes and got into my car. I told him that he could pay me for his trip to the airport whenever he returned to San Marcos and I gave him the sealed envelope. I told him, "This money is for you to use in case of an emergency. I expect that you will repay me in due time once you return to the United States." He promised and we continued to his destination.

Five weeks later, I get a call on my cell phone. It is Khalid calling and he tells me that he wants to treat me to the biggest entree at the Mexican restaurant near his apartment complex. We settled on meeting the next day for a big lunch. I picked him up the following day and we went for the big meal. When the drinks were served, he reached into his shirt pocket, took out an envelope and handed it to me, saying, "Please open this. It is for you." I opened the envelope and found a fifty dollar bill and two hundreds. I was paid in full. He reached into another pocket as I profusely thanked him for repaying me the loan. He said. "This gift is from my Mother. She is in awe of your generosity. See what the gift is." I opened the packet containing the gift and pulled out a small string of beads. Khalid tells me, "These prayer beads are the ones which my Mother has used every day since she was twelve years old. She wants you to have them." I was dumbstruck to think that a woman would let go of such a keepsake, giving it to a stranger. I was so impressed that I went home, took a large dream catcher from the wall in my den and went to Khalid's apartment to request that he send it to his Mother as my token of appreciation for her own generosity. I do believe that Khalid and I shall be friends for life as of this last encounter.

SOME PEOPLE ARE HARD TO PLEASE

I have failed to please some people who were my passengers, even though I have gone out of my way to add to their comfort while riding. I have received less than five stars from people who thought that I was driving too slow and those who thought I was driving too fast. I have received the same from those who thought it was great that I had information about eateries and other venues in the car and those who thought that it was shameful for me to provide such information.

MY TAKE ON THE AMERICAN PUBLIC

I have completed more that three thousand trips and have encountered more that twelve thousand passengers as of the time of my initial thought of writing this little book. The vast majority of passengers are Americans. My take on the American public is that we are a great people and our country is great. I am especially impressed with the caliber of people who are the new college-age students and the current young adult generation in America. Indeed, ninety-nine percent of my passengers have been interesting, interested, motivated, motivating, friendly and fun-loving individuals. They have a good sense of humor and they intend to care enough about others that this land is your land, this land is my land, from California to the New York islands, from the redwood forests to the Gulf stream waters. Truly they believe, 'this land is made for you and me'. People ask me sometimes as they ride with me, "What this driving has done for you personally". I tell them without hesitation that this driving HAS RESTORED MY FAITH IN THE AMERICAN PUBLIC! I do have doubts about the Pink Supremists, Klansmen, or the other sixty-two hate groups carousing around many parts of The State of Texas.

LITTLE INDIA

I have read in the past that major cities in America have neighborhoods which are populated by one or two peoples with the same ethnicity as the others around. There is 'little Italy', 'Chinatown", 'Little Polonia', and other such, in various regions of our country. Well, I am happy to announce, even to proclaim that San Marcos, Texas has its own 'little India'. This neighborhood is the apartment complex off of Sessom Drive at North LBJ Drive. I have been called numerous times for pick up by many international students who are enrolled in undergraduate and graduate programs at Texas State.

Several times, I have picked up a carload of students from either the southern part or the northern part of the country of India. They have always been talkative, friendly and courteous to me. They readily share that they are here to learn so that they may enter the business world as educated persons who will be a great success as an employee of a company somewhere in the world. I have taken them to buy a carload of groceries, return to the apartment complex with a trunk load of items of all kinds. I have taken them to see a great movie at the only movie theater in town. I have taken them to buy burgers, barbeque or other types of fast food. I have always been willing to wait while they made their purchases. Recently, one student gave me an invitation to her graduation ceremony. Another gave me an invitation to his traditional wedding ceremony, which will last four days and nights. I can barely wait to take part in those two event.

"WHERE CAN I GET SOME REALLY GOOD DRUGS?"

There have been occasions in which a passenger has asked me the question, "Where can I get some really good drugs?" I usually respond to them with an assurance that Austin is like most other communities in regards to really good drugs. I let the passenger know that Austin is famous for having places where passengers can stop by and get the drugs of their choice, sometimes with a big discount. I ask the passenger if he or she wants to go shopping now, since these little stop-ins are open day and night. Some people have taken me up on the offer. We get going and pretty soon I pull the car into the parking of an all-night CVS or Walgreen's and tell the passenger to go in and purchase the drugs of their choice. I will be glad to wait while they do their shopping. Most passengers do not think this is very funny.

"DO YOU CARE FOR SOME OF GRANDMAMA'S COOKIES?"

During my second month as a driver, I picked up a young man in downtown Austin around noon one weekday. He was carrying a backpack over his shoulder. I asked him for his destination and he told me that he was going to three different destinations and then coming back to the original pick up location.

We went to the first location which was a condo building near downtown but across the river. He got out and was gone about three minutes. I noticed when he returned to the car that the backpack seemed to contain fewer items. I asked whether he were a delivery man. He told me that he was delivering raisin cookies to customers who had ordered cookies by telephone from his grandmother. We made two more stops. After the third stopoff point, it appeared that the guy's backpack was totally empty. From this point, I drove him back to the original starting location. Too bad for me that I forgot to give him my telephone number or to ask for his or his grandmother's number. How in the blazes will I ever get an opportunity to get to taste grandmother's cookies? I was also disappointed that he did not offer me a chance to try some of grandma's cookies. It is also possible that the maker of the cookies goes by the nickname 'grandmama'.

'CHARLIE WHEELS'

Driving for RIDESHARE, especially at night and in the Austin, Texas region has its loads of dangers. There are many unlit streets, streets filled with speed bumps and curving roads with curbs that are in places I least expected to find them. There are also large holes in the fields around the Float Fest venue. I have had the misfortune of driving into a curb in an unlit area, in clear weather and in driving rainstorms, many times of day and night. I have driven through several pastures full of dust, dirt, rocks and big dips. I have befriended the owner and manager of Nichols Tire and Automotive in San Marcos, Texas because of these misadventures. The employees at Nichol's have patiently and quietly laughed as I drove into their parking lot and requested a new tire and a steel wheel to replace the aluminum wheel put on my car by the manufacturer. They endearingly gave me the nickname 'Charlie Wheels' in the early part of 2016 after I called on them to replace a wheel for the third time. At the time of this writing, they are doing my oil changes every five weeks since I am driving over nine hundred miles weekly in my part time work with RIDESHARE. Now they chuckle when I drive up to the building of their company and ask me first if I am here for an oil change or for another wheel for the car. I asked for some comments from them to use in the composition of this book and Fernando and Chris gave me the following:

'It is a pleasure to keep Charlie on the road!'

'RIDESHARE is a great activity to keep a retired person busy every week!'

'Retired people come in here for car service all of the time. Charlie is the only retired customer who has the latest style of cell phone. The rest of those people are still using the old cell phones that you have to flip open to use!'

'The frequency of Charlie's oil changes is outrageous!'

'Most of our customers use their car 5% of the day. Charlie uses his car 70% of the day!'

'Because of Charlie, we now have a large stock of steel wheels in our inventory!'

THE 'DUD' CALL TO WIMBERLEY

A 'dud' call happens when a driver receives a request for pick up, drives to the location of a passenger and finds that the passenger is no where to be found. My worst 'dud' call was from San Marcos to Wimberley. The trip one way was eighteen miles. I drove to the pick up location expecting that I would be taking the passenger on a lengthy trip and receive a healthy fare in return for my efforts, especially since I was apparently the only driver within twenty miles of Wimberley at the time. I drove through the center of Wimberley, out towards the high school and into the parking lot of a small convenience store. I stopped, called the passenger without getting a response to my call, and then circled the store. I got out of my car and went into to ask the clerk if someone had called for a ride. He told me that he did not see or hear anyone call for a ride. In fact, he had not had a customer in the store in the past forty-five minutes so he could not help me at all. What a dud! I wasted one full hour with the round trip and got nothing in return. Such is the occasional life of the RIDESHARE driver.

LAST CALL FOR ALCOHOL

It has happened more than once that passengers ask whether or not I am willing to serve alcohol in my car, since I regularly have ice cold water, candy or cookies to offer anyone. I do have an answer for passengers with that curiosity. I tell them that the liquor in my car is available after three in the morning. That is one hour after I give the last ride to RIDESHARE passengers. I get very few chuckles and a lot of moans from the people who ask for the last call for alcohol.

TOPLESS ON THE DRAG

People who travel in my RIDESHARE car are sometimes curious about the entertainment services available in the City of Austin. Brash passengers have asked whether there are any topless clubs in Austin and what is their location. I readily supply information on this matter. I also ask them if they wish to change their destination in the app and get a chance to see some of Austin's 'finest'. Next, I give the history of women going topless in Austin. I tell them that many topless women were walking the streets of the city when I first moved to Austin in late 1967. People who wanted to see the topless women did not have to pay to see the ladies. They merely had to take a drive or a walk down Guadalupe Street between 19th(now MLK) and 29th adjacent to the University of Texas at Austin campus. This area was fondly called the 'Drag' by the University population for many years. I tell them, "Some of those women were your Mothers, your Grandmothers and your Aunts. Those ladies had no idea that their openness could have generated a hefty income on a weekly basis. All they needed to do was to open a static display. Some people decided that this custom should stop taking place on the Drag and other people jumped at the opportunity to open places where people would pay dearly to see a 'dear lady' in the next to nothing. People now pay for what used to be free!!!

TELL US THE FUNNIEST THING YOU HAVE EVER DONE

A few times, my passengers have asked me to tell me the funniest thing I have done while I was driving. The funniest thing I have ever done as a driver was to tell the story of an interaction I had when I took a break from driving in San Marcos. I had an interaction with a very elderly woman one day in the local grocery market. We were in a long line. The woman was pushing the basket full of groceries directly behind me. The time was dragging because the people in front were buying basketsful of food. I got bored with all of the waiting and I turned around to the elderly woman and she asked "Young man, what is your age?" I looked at her rather angrily and I replied, "Lady, that is MY bidniz!" She smiled at me and she said to me, "Well, young fella, from the looks of things you have been in bidniz for a long time!" Ever since the day of this encounter I have never thought that I was doing a good job of hiding my age.

PET PEEVES

1. PET REFUSALS. The biggest peeve that I have as a RIDESHARE driver is to hear from a passenger that he or she has been refused a ride from a driver because the driver does not allow passengers to bring along any type of live animal or pet. I have had wonderful experiences when giving a ride to a passenger(s) who has along with them any kind of live animal, especially a cat or dog. I have made several trips to a veterinary office with a passenger who was taking a pet for vaccinations or because the pet was having symptoms of illness. On other occasions, I have given a ride to a passenger(s) who were going to the dog park or to the pool at Barton Springs which has a special place in the springs in which dogs are allowed to run free in the cool waters. The drivers who refuse such situations are obviously

driving a leased car under a contract which prohibits transport of any kind of live animal. There could also be the case that the driver has a fear or dislike of live animals. One rider in my car had his special dog with him to give aid because his master was sight-impaired. I loved that the dog came along. That dog weighed at least one hundred and twenty pounds. He got in before his master, stretched across the floorboard and sat quietly for the entire trip. He was no problem, but a pure joy to have along for the ride. I have heard on two occasions from sight-impaired passengers that they were refused a ride by two or three other drivers prior to my acceptance of their request for a pick up. The drivers who have refused must not be aware that it is against the law to refuse to transport a sight-impaired passenger who has their special dog along with them as a necessity. I am open to the possibility of transporting a passenger who is carrying any non-vicious animal or serpent. Honestly, I look forward to giving a ride to a passenger who has with them a defanged cobra, coral, copperhead or rattlesnake. The only critter which gives me the 'heebie jeebies' is the scorpion. Please do not request a ride from my RIDESHARE car if you plan to travel in the company of a scorpion.

2. I always get peeved when a passenger gets upset about the fact that I carry brochures about businesses and events in the bucket area inside of my car. I want my passengers to have information about excellent and fun services and events in my area. I am willing to provide such information at no charge to the owners of restaurants, bars, dance halls and other types of service locations. I do this at my own pleasure and inside of my own personal vehicle. Several passengers submitted an observation after riding in my car in the past three years that they did not appreciate that I was pushing business for other people in my area. To be perfectly honest, I do not appreciate the fact that some passengers do not approve of the fact that I am free inside of my own personal vehicle to provide the printed material of my choice.

3. I do not appreciate that people from other states, especially and particularly from the east coast, get upset because they did not like the style of service presented to them by the owners and employees of barbecue establishments in the Austin region. Several have commented to me and to their fellow passengers that they thought it was 'cheap' for an eatery to serve barbecue and the fixings on a sheet of butcher paper. Well, my dear readers, this is the way the true cookers and vendors of barbeque in central Texas present their finished product. It has always been this way and it shall always be this way. I want to make the point that the barbecue from these eateries is of the highest quality. It is even 'finger-licking' good. Be sure to lick the barbecue sauce off of your fingers while you are eating this gourmet barbecue in the best serving format at the best establishments in central Texas. It is proper for me to say here and to tell people who call the eateries 'cheap' that the butcher paper that is being used has been produced by a Texas company by the name of 'Carne Butcher Paper Production Company'. This butcher paper is especially prepared and preserved with special spices in it which offer wonderful flavor to the paper when the barbecue is served on it. So, people do have something else new to learn about the great State of Texas when they ride in my car and make observations about Texas barbecue. I hope that every reader of this episode has had or will one day have an opportunity to eat barbecue that is served on butcher paper that was produced and delivered to the eatery by The Carne Company. The aroma of this specially prepared and served barbecue is exquisite in flavor. It is finger-licking' good. Just be sure that after finishing your meal you do not try to take the butcher paper home to show your friends and neighbors who live in the eastern part of The United States and have not enjoyed the flavors of butcher paper barbecue.

MY BIGGEST BENEFITS FROM DRIVING FOR RIDESHARE

I have received an untold amount of benefits in my three years of driving for rideshare companies in the Austin, Texas region.

1. The greatest benefit for me has been to find that driving passengers in the Austin region is not work at all. People ask me all of the time how I like this job. I must say that I cheerfully tell them that this is not a job at all and that once this feels like a job I will resign on the spot. I do promise that, when I get that feeling, should I have passengers I will not resign until those people have been safely transported to their intended destination. Please do not have the worry that one day you might be the passenger who has the misfortune of being in my car when I get the feeling of this being a job. I solemnly promise!!!

2. A second benefit is that I have loved the extra income. It is not an exorbitant amount, since I drive on a part time basis. I generally average twenty-eight hours on the road weekly. There are some weeks during which I drive seventy hours. That occurs during the happenings in Austin of Austin City Limits and South By Southwest. The extra income means that I have not had to change my life style in any way since I retired from a job of forty-four years. The extra income allows me and my wife the chance to travel to San Diego, California for a four-night vacation. It allows us to go to nice restaurants weekly and to buy meats from the 'gourmet' counter at the local grocery store. I have acquired a special taste for rib eyes, t-bones and New York cuts. Now, I can buy bottles of delicious merlot, cabernet savignon and chianti from the more expensive racks in the liquor outlets. I am now able to pay for everyone's meals when we get together with a few friends in a nice eatery. These freedoms mean a lot to me.

3. Another benefit is that I am able to make a monthly contribution to the education fund which I began in my first month of driving.

It is to the benefit of my one and only great granddaughter, Daisy Juanita. I must say that she is the apple of my eye and that of my wife's eye also. This 'little apple' is only four years of age this year and I hope she will be able to have some education money in the bank when she enrolls in a university. The account should make some interest on the balance every month for the next fifteen years and amount to several thousand dollars for her to use. The total will never cover all of her expenses, but it will be an extra few thousand dollars for which she will not have to work. This fund should help her to focus on studies alone.

4. A fourth benefit is that I have been able to meet so many people from all walks of life and from so many countries around the world. In my capacity as a driver in the Austin region, I have been very much an ambassador and tour guide to people who are here on business, for entertainment and for time to look for a place to live in the city or in surrounding suburbs. My observation of the make-up of other drivers is that the vast majority of them are new to Austin. Many of them are immigrants to America, who have names differing from those to which I am accustomed. The vast majority of them are driving cars which are totally unmarked. I believe that they are driving leased vehicles which they must not decorate in any form. Many of my passengers have related that most of their drivers are not familiar with the streets, with the locations of businesses and places of entertainment, and are totally uneducated about the history of the illustrious city which is Austin, Texas. I drive my own car and I decorate it regularly with bumper stickers on the rear of my car. I have enjoyed, most of all, finding out where people are from, where they have visited in other parts of the world and telling them about my few adventures to other parts of the world. I believe that I have done more than my part to make people welcome to our city and to know that they are going to have an enjoyable visit because they are in the 'heart' of southern hospitality.

Some passengers are curious to know what I did for a living before I got into the ride-sharing business. Since I am proud of the work which I did for fifty-three years before retiring and driving, I am eager to share the joys which I found in my earlier professions. I take the time to share that I have done numerous things to make a decent living after college graduation. I have been in ministry as a clergyman. I have been a political activist. I have been a campaign manager twice for a relative who won races for a judgeship in central Texas. I have been the director of a residential program for boys who failed in the state foster system. I have been a grant writer. I serve as a member of The Board of Directors for a cultural center and for a center which houses services for people with mental challenges.

MY BUCKET LIST

I enjoy sharing with passengers some of the contents on my bucket list.

My friends, I must tell you this. The items on my bucket list are coming true. I once had on the top of my list a wish that I live to be witness to a winner of The Triple Crown of thoroughbred racing. I am happy to say that the wish came true in July 2015 when American Pharoah was the winner of The Belmont Stakes and Triple Crown.

My wish to be at the High School graduation of my great granddaughter, Daisy Juanita, is what tops the list at this time.

Secondly, I wish to attend a traditional wedding of a couple of Indian descent, whether they celebrate in the U.S. or in India.

Thirdly, I wish to be the first RIDESHARE driver in America to be driving while wearing Depends." I told this list to a passenger once, and she wanted to know if I were driving this trip while wearing Depends. I assured her that my wish would not come true for a long time.

Fourth on the list is my goal of winning the lottery, purchasing a Lamborghini SUV, and taking my passengers around in the best style possible. Anyone in the region is eligible for this ride, since I will have the auto listed as a 'basic class' vehicle.

Most passengers tell me that I will experience all of these wishes.

MY BACKGROUND CHECK

My ride sharing company exited from the city limits of Austin, Texas in 2016, so I decided that I would join another company who had agreed to have all drivers obtain a fingerprint background check. This was a matter of compliance with an Austin, Texas city ordinance. I did the assigned task, even attaching the decal of proof of fingerprint check onto my front windshield. Passengers began asking the meaning of the decal on the window almost immediately. One person was so brash as to ask if that were a copy of my actual fingerprint. I still tell inquiring passengers that I have made up a funny story about the day on which I received written notice of the results of my fingerprint check. "The report stated that when I was nine years of age I had been prosecuted and convicted of stealing ten cents worth of bubble gum(ten separately-wrapped pieces back in those days) in a court of law in Houston, Texas. The judge fined me twenty-five cents for the theft and required that I pay the court costs of one dollar and seventeen cents. This report was the only one I received." I assure the passengers who hear the story that it is in no way the truth, but is a spoof on the folly of any driver needing to get a fingerprint background check in order to be deemed fit to transport the public.

A TALE FOR PEOPLE FROM ATLANTA

I often give rides to passengers who are visiting Austin, Texas from Atlanta, Georgia. I have shared with them that I once had a business when I lived in Houston, Texas. I was eleven years of age. My Mom had forbidden me to cross any street, so I was confined to the sidewalks on all four sides of a huge square block. I decided that I would use my little red wagon to go into business for myself. I managed in a matter of weeks to knock on the front door of every house on the block(s). I requested of the inhabitants of each home that they save all of their old newspapers (The Houston Chronicle, The Houston Post and The Houston Press). I promised to come by weekly for the papers they saved for me. On one afternoon, I would load the garage full of newspapers into Mom's car and have her drive me to the public scale on Washington Avenue. We would weigh the car with the papers inside, pull up to a dumpster and unload the car, and then re-weigh the car without papers inside. The scale owners paid for old papers by the pound. I usually was paid four dollars for a carload. I took the money, gave two dollars to Mom, put one dollar in my piggy bank and went to the neighborhood grocery store around the corner (Butera's) and bought one dollar's worth of candy, sodas and twenty baseball cards. The cards came one to a packet, with a piece of Topp's bubble gum inside. One afternoon, I slowly opened each packet. I happened upon the rookie baseball card of Henry Aaron, or Hammerin' Hank, as the fans were already nicknameing him. He was a star player on the baseball team, The Milwaukee Braves, and move with the team to Atlanta where he continued to become a man of great fame. I submitted to my listeners that the card is still in uncirculated condition and worth at least four thousand dollars. A one penny investment turned a four thousand percent return. Of course, I have the card locked in a safety deposit box.

The first part of the previous story is what I tell to visitors from Chicago as well. The story changes when I get to the part about opening one of the twenty cards and finding the rookie card of Ernie Banks, known for years as Mr. Cub. This card is also still in uncirculated condition. It has a value of at lest five thousand dollars. That one cent investment has returned five thousand percent, or greater, since Ernie passed away in 2016. Naturally, that card also is in the safety deposit box.

A TALE FOR PEOPLE FROM SAN FRANCISCO

This tale is about a gift to me from my Father-in-law(now deceased). He was visiting the City of San Francisco in the week in which the Giants played their first baseball games after moving from the east coast. He had a great love for the game, so he was able to get a baseball autographed by most of the Giants' players. He gave me that baseball, which I cherish and keep in a very safe place. Some signatures have faded, but two of the most important ones are still readable. They are the signatures of Hal Lanier and Juan Marichal.Most people from San Francisco do not have such a collectors' item and they tell me so. The ones who are baseball fans tell me to hold onto that item for as long as I can.

THE REAL MANCHACA

The true and original name of Manchaca is "Menchaca". The true name is an hispanic name. The original namers of the community of Manchaca were hispanic people who honored a family in said community by giving it their last name. English speakers, some of whom were given to naming roads and communities and street signs as well used their own understanding and Anglo pronunciation to name the street and the community of MANCHACA. The street and the community are commonly referred to as MANCHAK!!! You are now riding in my car on Manchak Street as we travel towards or away from the community of Manchak!!!

THE REAL BUDA

There is no such thing as Budda, Texas. Nor is there a Bu'dder, Texas. The name Buda was given to the town directly south of Austin, Texas by Anglo town-namers who favored the name which they personally chose. This was in lieu of continuing to use the original name given by hispanics living in the vicinity. Ages ago, when the first railroad came south from Austin, this community was no community at all. It was the site of a large water tower put there by the owners of the railroad. The train stopped to fill the water tank car of the train with a fresh supply for the steam engine to use in its journeys. In those days, there was only one home within sight of the tower. It was a wood frame structure occupied by two widows who had immigrated from Mexico. The members who lived nearby the home dearly called the whistle stop of the train 'viuda', which is the spanish word for widow. The spanish pronunciation is bee-yu'-da. Hence, the arrival of the word 'buda'. Sometimes, I jokingly tell my passengers that we are approaching 'bu-da-da' as we get into the city limits of Buda, Texas.

THE VIEW OF THE STATE CAPITOL

I am quite proud to live near a city in this nation which has a capitol building. I make a point of telling visitors to Austin that a good way to spend some time in the city is to take a walk or tour through the capitol building, knock on the door of a legislator or senator and ask for a short visit to learn about state government, and to read the information printed on manuscripts and statues which adorn the building and the grounds. I tell them that when I first moved to Austin in 1967, ordinances prohibited the construction of tall buildings around the capitol. The ordinances were the attempt by people in power to be sure that anyone could see the capitol anytime day or night from as far away as five miles. I submit to them that the ordinances were in effect until developers got the ears of the people in power in the city and state and convinced them to remove the ordinances in the name of growth and progress.

THE 'COLORADO' RIVER

In my trips around Austin, Texas, I have taken the opportunity to tell passengers the story of how The Colorado River' has defied the geography and topography of America. It is definitely a fact of nature that the real Colorado River flows through Arizona. It reaches no where close to Texas, much less Austin, Texas. I explain that the original mapmakers of this region of The United States were of hispanic origin and spoke only spanish. Their initial and original intention was to name The Red River. However, any student of geograpahy who passed their class with at least a 'C' knows, The Red River does not flow through the center of Texas. It is the grand and glorious river that divides Texas and Oklahoma. As well, the spanish name for 'red' is COLORADO!!!

TEXAS A&M IN THE 1950'S EQUALS TRAINS, JOHN DAVID CROW, YALE LARY, JACK PARDEE AND ONE-ARMED ELMENDORF

This is the story I always tell to passengers who let me know that they attended Texas A&M at College Station. I tell the passengers that my grandparents were born in Poggio Reale, Sicily and immigrated to Bryan-College Station, Texas in the 1880s. People ask why they came to Texas. I tell them that the people from the small village were invited by four American farmers from Texas to come and help them to grow cotton beautifully. The descendants of those Sicilian families are wealthy people today because eventually they were able to purchase river bottom farm land for growing cotton all along the Brazos River from College Station to Waco. Not only that, but the 'Aggie' scientists developed long-stem cotton. They made it possible for the cotton farmers to grow three times as many cotton bowls per stem, translating into three times the wealth per acre as before the discovery of the longer stem.

I made a wise decision to join the Boy Scouts when I was in Bryan. The troop met weekly and got to usher football games at Kyle Field on the fifty yard line. All of us scouts in Troop 183 would arrive with our Scout Masters at least two hours before game time. Mr. Bolmanski was the lead Master. He owned a photography studion and made his living taking graduation pictures from Aggie seniors wearing fine military dress boots and holding long swords. The second Master was Mr. Zubik. He made his living making senior boots for the graduating Aggies.

We scouts would go to the top row of seats of the stadium and watch as the trains arrived in THE COLLEGE STATION, bringing people to the game in about twenty passenger cars per train from as far away as Houston and Dallas. Friends, this short story lets you know the history of the naming of the town in which you find the main campus of The University of Texas A&M system.

There were several notables on the team when I did the ushering. Jack Pardee was the quarterback. He eventually became the head coach for the Houston Oilers. John David Crow was the running back. He is the first winner of The Heisman Trophy from Texas A&M. On the offensive line there was a one-armed guard by the name of Elmendorf. The field goal kicker was Yale Lary. He graduated from the University and got the job of kicker for The Cleveland Browns, where he succeded Leo 'The Toe' Groza, a player who is in the Hall of Fame. HALLA BALLO, KINEK, KINEK!!

GETTING A BANK LOAN IN THE 1960S

Some of my passengers have asked me to tell them about the economic and racial discrepancies I saw back in the 1960s. I tell them that I began my Austin, Texas experience in August 1967. I moved from Houston, Texas to begin work as an assistant pastor at a church on the east side of the city. The only anglo people to live in this part of Austin were people who worked in churches. The neighborhood was hispanic from East Seventh Street, to the east of the trenches that would be come Interstate Highway 35 and going south to the Colorado River. There were no stop signs on Holly Street, nor on East First Street(now Cesar Chavez Street). East of the trenches under construction and to the north of East Seventh Street, the neighborhood was populated exclusively by people of African-American descent. This 'territory' was unfondly referred to by residents of other parts of the city as 'east Austin'. There was little to no businesses in the area. There were no banks at all. I recall that a few friends from the 'east side' opened up a minority bank because people living in 'east Austin' never qualified for a home loan nor for a home improvement loan. This bank was on the east access of the Interstate between Eleventh Street and Twelfth Street.

THE ROOTS OF 'DIRTY' SIXTH STREET

Sixth Street is referred to these days as 'dirty Sixth'. In the good old days, there was no such designation. Sixth Street to the east of the trenches that were becoming Interstate Highway 35 was referred to as the locale of bars called 'shooting galleries'. These were places where the windows of a drinking establishment were boarded up from the inside for a very good reason. The boards were there to provide for the safety of people walking or driving on the street. Boards were nailed up to keep the bullets from getting outside of the establishments. I recall that on any Saturday night, one to three men met their maker when they were victims of 'venganza'. It was my good or bad fortune to be a young assistant pastor at a church in east Austin in those days. One church of my denomination was much closer to Brackenridge

Emergency Room. The church was served by two old geezers who must have retired for the night as early as eight pm. They never answered the phone when a nurse called for a minister to come and give the 'last rites' to a dying patient. I will always recall my first call to the emergency room. It was during my first week in Austin. The call came to my bedside about two in the morning. The person calling me identified herself as an emergency room nurse at Brackenridge Hospital. She said that she was trying to care for a shooting victim who just arrived in an ambulance from an establishment near Sixth and Waller. I jumped out of bed, dressed in two minutes, got into my car and rushed down Holly to the construction area that is now the east access road. I was at the emergency room very quickly. The nurse met me at the door, led me into a cubby hole where there was a man on a stretcher. He was bare chested and there were at least a dozen little holes showing on his chest. I almost fainted at the sight. I decided to follow the procedures I had learned in my training. I asked the required first question of an awake but supposedly dying person. I asked in Spanish, "Do you wish to confess yourself". Hah! Was I in for a surprise. The guy looked at me and in plain English, replied, "Hell, no. I ain't confessin' nuthin."

I always assure my passengers that there is no need for them to duck down onto the running boards of my car as we pass down any east Austin streets in these days. Streets are almost totally safe since the Austin Police Department provides vigilance in a healthy manner both day and night.

THE HISTORY OF RAINEY STREET

Many Austin people like to spend an evening in The Rainey Street entertainment district. Some are locals; some are touring the city. Almost none of these people know the history of this city district. All of them want to hear something from me as we travel to the area. I am able to tell them that the district was an hispanic area when I first moved here in 1967. I let them know that the poorest of the poor of the city lived in the remodeled homes they are soon to visit for the afternoon or evening. I tell them that the only productive business around was the company called Roy's Taxi. I explain that in those days I was a member of The St. Vincent de Paul Society and made many visits to homes on Rainey Street in response to residents' calls to my office requesting financial help for paying rent, utilities, a doctor bill or car payment. Some requested help with food vouchers. I visited these homes when I got a call, accompanied by Pete Velasquez or Julio Teran. We visited in order to affirm the validity of the request. Eventually, the residents were replaced when they sold their properties for a large amount of money to wealthy entrepreneurs. These buyers have been making fancy entertainment venues and condo buildings by doing massive remodel or demolition jobs. The neighborhood is no longer the same. The term for these transactions dates to the 1960s government program called 'Urban Renewal', which was unfondly called 'Chicano Removal' by those who were activists for minority groups in Austin in those days.

JOURNAL ENTRIES

The comments which you are about to read are the comments entered into three large journals which I carried in my ride-sharing car for people to make written comments of any kind.

"Charles is so awesome-a wealth of Austin hot spots! This is the best place to be(riding in his car) for tour information. If you ever come to Couer d' Alene, Idaho, Charlie, you look me up and I will share our hot spots. Thanks so much." Kristi

"Charlie, you know amazing things. Thanks for the ride and the education." Heather, from Michigan

"I'm on my way to work and would rather die. But, thanks for giving me your favorite places in San Marcos that I didn't even know about. And you made me laugh. So thanks for making my morning a little better". Kylie

"Charlie, I'm Vanessa. Thank you very much for an entertaining ride. Me agrado mucho que hables espanol y que nos compartirnos sus experiencias en mexico. Muchas gracias por los dulces y pan!!"

"Charlie. When you go to Rio, make sure you go to Leblon and Urca". Paula, Fatima, y Katharina, from Brazil.

"It was great meeting you. Thanks for the ride. Your energy is contagious." Love, Laeticia, from Cueritiba, PR, Brazil

"Charlie, I have a nephew named Charlie. I love him and I love you. Sorry about the bad handwriting. If anyone that's good-looking reads this and is single, call me. (210)725-83--." (unsigned).

"Thank you for a great ride and all the graphics. I loved hearing about the history of the area. A great ride, with great Texas hospitality." Melissa, from Atlanta

"Thanks for driving during SXSW. Thanks for driving in the crappy traffic and the rain." Andrew, from California

"Put me in the book". Logan

"First night back in San Marcos for the school year". Bryce

"Charlie, in fact you never know whom you might meet; absolute pleasure meeting you". Bernie

"I know that some drivers top 6,000 trips. But, you were more than a trip! A friend. Thanks!

These people were on the way to Float Fest:

"We're on the way to Float Fest to go see Cage the Elephant". Signed, (at various times and on various trips to the river).

Katie, VCSB, Go Gauchos!

Pilar, NYU, Go Violets!

Saey, UT, Go Horns!

Chloe, SU, Go Bulldogs!

Clayton, TAMU, Go Aggies!

DRIVERS, PACK YOUR CAR WITH NECESSITIES

There are certain items which must be available to passengers in a Rideshare car. Here is my short list. It is the list of items which have proven to be useful and to be enjoyable for passengers.

1. Paper sacks. These are for various situations. Certainly passengers need a bag when they are feeling sick in the stomach after a late night out on the town. This is a money-saving procedure for an ill passenger. Failure to use the paper bag may result in a three hundred dollar bill sent by the company for the cleaning of a 'passenger mess' inside the car. Paper bags are also useful as well for the collection of trash items. This helps the driver to keep the inside of the car in excellent tidy condition. All drivers love to receive the comment that their car is neat and clean.

2. Paper towels. These items are good for cleaning the inside and outside of every window before and during the work day. Also, some passengers ride in the car with sticky fingers. They sometimes

get sticky fingers from licking on the candies provided by a caring driver.

3. Hand wipes. These items are better than paper towels because they often have a damp feature which makes for easy wiping. All passengers enjoy easy wipes while they are passing over the terribly rough streets of Austin, especially Guadalupe Street.

4. First Aid Kit.
   All sorts of people use ride-sharing for their transportation at this time. Some of them feel just fine. They ride home after finishing a great meal, getting a 'buzz' from a night and early morning from local bars, or they have a good 'tired' from a long day or night of clean, hard work. There are also some passengers who have need of the contents of a first aid kit. They ask for contents from a first aid kit for broken fingernails, cuts on their fingers or arms, and all other sorts of minor injuries. Drivers get great appreciation when they can respond to a request for some help by saying, "I have just what you need. Just pop open the glove compartment and take what you need".

5. Assorted Candy. Passengers especially appreciate that a driver is thoughtful enough to put some candy munchies in his car for their enjoyment on their trip to a destination. The good ole public sometimes is able to let loose and show the child in them. They are happy to see tootsie rolls, suckers of all flavors, chocolate minis, and peppermint sticks and small round pieces of the same when they look around the car. Every year at Halloween I am sure to pack in some treats for everyone. At that time, I add licorice sticks to the mix and my passenger go for it vigorously. Passengers arriving at the airport after a long flight cannot wait to get their hands on the candy in my car when I offer it to them. They exclaim that it has been hours since they had a decent meal and they are delighted that I carry goodies for both little and big kids.

6. Bottles of cold water. Passengers appreciate this necessity especially after two in the morning after a night out at the bars.

7. Cell phone cords. This is an urgent necessity, especially since most people forget to bring their own cord or they forgot to charge their phone. This is a priority item, forgotten in front of remembering to bring personal identification, credit cards, feeding the cat or the dog, or bringing the husband or wife.

8. Maps of the city. This is helpful for the tourists, since most people have no idea of the layout of the city.

9. A journal for notes from the passengers. Most people tell me that my having a journal is the best idea they have heard for having in a vehicle. I use journals to get comments in any language. My journals have comments, with an English translation, from people representing more than thirty different countries. A couple from Tel Aviv rode with me once and the husband did a paragraph in his language, but forgot to translate it. So, now I am seeking a Rabbi for help with the entry.

10. Note pad and pens. Some people still enjoy writing notes on a pad. They eagerly use my materials when I give them a list of venues of interest in our city. Some of them get the info when they are enroute to the airport and intend to use the notes upon return at a future date. Some take down my email in case they want to enlarge the list at a later date.

11. List of current events in the city. I make a point of reading the entertainment columns in the newspapers from Austin and San Marcos. So, I have a mental list of most of the action available currently and in coming weeks in the city. Passengers love this.

12. A working car radio. Every Rideshare driver in the Austin region should be required to have a SIRIUS XM radio system, in working

condition, in the car. I have SIRIUS I, SIRIUS II AND SIRIUS III in my car. However, I always play the same channel for my passengers. Numerous people have asked if my car brought in other channels. I have replied that I tried other channels on four occasions. Each time I got off of the one channel, the wires to my radio self-destructed. The station which I always play is Channel 59. That is the channel which plays WILLIE'S ROADHOUSE. It is broadcast from Nashville in the mornings and from Austin from early afternoon until midnight. This is the channel of Wilie Nelson, the music icon of traditional western music. It is CHANNEL 59, OR BUST!!!

It is appropriate for me to say in this book that ride-sharing is here to stay. This newer mode of transportation for people from almost all countries in the world is the cheapest and most efficient means available for everyone who uses it. This new model has given new life to older people who need the income from a safe part time activity. It has taken dangerous drivers off of the road at hours when visibility is close to zero, especially in the middle of the night. This new mode has given us a new generation of recreational drinkers of alcoholic beverages who have sworn to all of us ride-sharing drivers that they will never get behind the wheel of their car ever again after drinking alcohol. The services of ride-sharing companies and the commitment of people who drink and will never drive afterward gives all of us safer streets and highways. This gives a safe means of transportation back home to thousands of young women in America who work in the late night venues of fast food locations. It has been means of rapid and inexpensive transportation to individuals and families who need to get to a hospital emergency room or other location where they have access to basic needs not available at home. I say to all users of ride-sharing services, This new mode of transportation also helps to reduce the number of vehicles off of streets and highways, replacing the current congestion many of us face in and around our cities. "Enjoy your ride, your driver and a safe life from now on!"